Star of Wonder

A Walk with God

Leena Susan Chacko

BookLeaf Publishing
India | USA | UK

Made with ❤ on the BookLeaf Publishing Platform
www.bookleafpub.in
www.bookleafpub.com

Dedication

This book I dedicate to my dearest Daddy, whose passion for the English language has been the spark behind my own. Thank you for nurturing my love for words, for showing me the joy hidden in every sentence and for teaching me how language can be as playful as it is powerful.

To my cherished Mummy, thank you for teaching me the power of prayer and for your unwavering dedication to my education. Your insistence on mastering English wasn't always easy, but it was your gift to me, one that taught me discipline, resilience and a hunger for excellence. The countless hours you spent guiding me, believing in my potential even when I doubted myself, have shaped who I am.

Together, you both have given me wings – Daddy, the wings to explore and play with words, and Mummy, the wings of faith and discipline that ground and uplift me.

With all my love and gratitude,

Your daughter, Leena

Acknowledgements

'Give thanks to the Lord, for He is good; His steadfast love endures forever'! – Psalm 118:1

First and foremost, I give thanks to God, whose unending love and grace have been my foundation and the source of every word in this collection. His mercy and presence made this journey of faith possible.

To my husband, thank you for your steady support and strength, which have helped me persevere.

To my dear sisters and their families, your love, prayers and encouragement have been a source of comfort and strength.

To my cherished friend Maria, your friendship and faith have been a true gift, inspiring and uplifting me throughout this journey.

May God bless each of you abundantly, for you have all played a vital role in bringing this collection to life.

With heartfelt gratitude
Leena Susan Chacko

Preface

'I have been crucified with Christ; it is no longer I who live, but Christ who lives in me'. – Galatians 2:20

Star of Wonder – A Walk with God is more than a book; it's a journey written from the depths of my soul, capturing the moments where my heart and faith have been tested, healed and renewed by the One who calls us each by name. In every line and stanza, you will find echoes of my own pilgrimage – moments of searching, glimpses of light and encounters with grace that have marked my path with Jesus as my constant companion.

The title, Star of Wonder, symbolises that brilliant light of faith that has guided me through both the darkest valleys and the brightest peaks. Like the wise men who followed a star to discover the newborn King, I, too, have sought to walk closely with Him, navigating life's uncertainties with my gaze fixed on His love and mercy. This book is an offering of the insights, joys and even struggles that have deepened my walk with Christ, drawing me ever nearer to His heart.

These poems are meant to uplift and inspire, to remind us that each step in faith, no matter how small, brings us closer to the One who loves us beyond measure. As you journey through these pages, my prayer is that you, too, will feel His presence – His love, His strength, His gentle guidance – just as I have.

This collection, I hope, will be a guiding star for you, dear reader, illuminating the path that leads not only to faith but to an intimate, enduring relationship with our Saviour. Wherever you are in your own journey, may these words remind you that He walks with you, every step of the way.

In the love of Christ and His Church,
Leena Susan Chacko

A Reason To Live

He kept coming after me, never to forsake me.
He kept coming, even if I had forsaken Him.
His heart wept when I decided to give up,
yet He stayed close, even when I had turned away.
Whispering my name when I would not hear it,
waiting for the day I would recognise His voice.
His merciful eyes were on the lookout for me,
on those days when I was lost and wandered,
thinking I could manage alone.
But still, He waited – patient, kind and true,
His love never fading, no matter what I do.
Then, in an instant, His arms were around me,
not with anger, but with endless grace.
It is then I realised my nothingness and
the emptiness that I carried without His embrace.
I came back to Him, broken yet whole,
for in His mercy, He restored my soul.
Now I have found a reason to live–
to live for my Saviour, who died for me.
In His love, I have found my way,
and in His grace, I will forever stay.
No treasure on Earth could match His embrace,
no fleeting joy could ever replace the peace I have
found in His loving gaze.
Through valleys of shadow, He is my light.

Through every darkness, He holds me tight.
When the world deceives and hope seems small,
He is the one who catches my fall.
He fills every void, heals every ache,
mends every scar for His love's sake.
Now I walk each day with a joyful heart,
learning from His love I will never part.
In His arms, I am finally free,
redeemed and restored eternally.

Thank You, Lord

A word or two is just not enough, yet too many
words would spoil it.
It is just from my heart to Yours that beats a
simple 'Thank You'.
The immense blessings, Your unfathomable love
and Your mercy are beyond what I can
comprehend.
Each sunrise, each breath – a gift I do not deserve,
yet You pour them out without end.
In the stillness of the night, when I am alone,
I feel Your presence, reminding me I am never on
my own.
I am overwhelmed by Your grace, so freely given,
and in this moment, I know I am forgiven.
In the end, Lord, I feel so unworthy to say just a
'Thank You'.
But I know too many said words would spoil it.
So from my heart to Yours, will always beat
'Thank You'.
When the world is loud and I lose my way,
You gently pull me back, and in Your arms, I stay.
No words can measure the depth of my praise,
but with every beat of my heart, Your name I will
raise.

For every gift, for every trial, You have carried me through,
Lord, my soul will forever whisper, 'Thank You'.

A Heart Fully Surrendered

My Saviour, my King and my Guide,
let my life be to You a pleasing sacrifice.
To You, my life, I totally surrender.
Let me worship You in all glory and splendour.
Be in me a consuming fire,
consuming my body, mind and soul
and each and every desire.
Then I will be made completely whole.
Do to me what You please,
for I am only Yours, Yours alone.
Like the clay on the potter's wheel,
all my plans I lay at Your feet.
Health I will not ask, wealth I will not seek.
But to be drawn closer to You, is all that I please.
In Your love, I find my peace,
in Your presence, my worries cease.
Guide my steps on this journey of grace,
with You, my Lord, I find my place.
Help me serve others with a heart so true,
reflecting the light that comes only from You.
In every moment, let me sing Your praise,
in every breath, may my spirit blaze.

In Line With Your Love

As I wake up to go to church,
let me make an effort to be in line
with Your love, Your thoughts, Your gentle touch,
that leads me from shadow to light divine.

Teach me, Lord, in every stride,
to walk in grace, to see what's true,
to cast aside my restless pride,
and find my peace alone in You.

Help me listen as the hymns arise,
to words that heal, to prayers that mend.
Let my heart open, unwise to lies,
and find in faith the truest friend.

With each step towards Your sacred place,
I lay my worries, my cares, my fears.
To feel Your mercy, to sense Your grace,
and wipe away unspoken tears.

Teach me to see as You would see,
with kindness as my daily guide.
To bear Your image humbly, free,
with love and truth in step beside.

So as I sit within these pews,
a soul among so many here,
I lift my heart; my soul renews
with every whispered, grateful prayer.

Let this journey draw me near,
to know You more, to seek Your will.
And in Your presence, calm and clear,
find strength to climb life's rising hill.

My Soul Magnifies The Lord

My soul magnifies you, Lord, in awe,
as Mary's words become my own.
For You have seen me in my weakness,
and lifted me up from the unknown.

In my humble days, You have shown me grace,
a love so vast, it fills my soul.
I, like Mary, am small and lowly,
yet in Your plan, You make me whole.

You scatter pride and raise the meek,
bringing light where shadows lay.
You fill the hungry with endless gifts
and guide my steps along Your way.

When life's burdens feel too heavy,
I remember her song, her trust, her peace.
Her faith reminds me to surrender
and in Your mercy, find release.

For You, my Saviour, are my strength,
a faithful God, both firm and kind.
As Mary's heart rejoiced in You,
I find my joy in the grace I find.

With each day, Lord, let me sing,
of Your mercy that never departs.
My spirit magnifies Your name,
as I hold Your promise in my heart.

Grace In The Struggle

I am not very good at keeping a happy face
with the cross that I am carrying.
It is too heavy for me, Lord,
though I know it is you who is carrying it for me.
I am not very good at praising You,
when all I see is the troubles that surround me.
It is too many to count, Lord,
though I know that it is nothing compared to
what You have gone through.
I will not ask You why,
and I will only try,
to trust in Your understanding,
though I cannot figure out anything.
I will try; just give me the grace
to look at trouble in the face,
with a smile on my face and
a praise on my lips always.
When my knees buckle and my strength fades,
Lord, remind me of the price You paid.
When doubts rise and shadows fall,
help me remember You endured it all.
I may not have all the answers clear,
but with You, Lord, I have no need to fear.
For in every trial, Your love prevails,
even when my human heart fails.

So I will walk this path, though weary and weak,
for in my struggle, it is Your grace I seek.
With faith in my heart, I will press ahead,
trusting in You, just as You have said.

A Leap Of Faith

A huge leap of faith
is what You are asking me to do.
No looking back, no glancing forward,
just following Your statutes and holding Your guiding hand.
Scary at times, overwhelming all the time,
to let go of my comfort and face the unknown.
What lies ahead of me, I do not know.
At this moment, all I see is You.
Never let a moment pass without You.
Never let Your grace and mercy be away from me.
Never let Your back be turned against me,
for I have no one but only You.
Just give me the grace to see every day Your face,
my soul's delight, my strength and might.
For You, let my personal dreams be crushed to the ground,
so Your work can continue in me, all my life.
For my only desire is to please only You.
In each shadow that comes, let me still find Your light,
in the silence, let me hear Your voice, so bright.
When my heart trembles and the fear fails to subside,
remind me that You are there, always by my side.

Though I falter, Lord, hold me strong
in Your love, where I forever belong.
With You, I will take this leap again,
my faith will be anchored in You till the very end.

One More Chance

Just one more chance Lord give me,
as this new year dawns to its first glory.
Let me hold Your hands daily
so all the way, You can lead me
through Your grace and mercy.
That is all I ask of You,
my Lord and everlasting King,
and I belong solely to You.

The last year, You made me strong
through all my ups and downs.
Though some roads turned up wrong,
You were there with me all along.
Without You, I would not have been able to go on.
Without You, I would be all lost and forlorn.
But You, my Lord, lifted me up on Your throne
and thenceforth, I was never alone.

Today Lord, when I look back,
I see many of my setbacks.
But You Lord, put me on the right track.
When things were tough, You carried me on Your back.
Thank You Lord, for being there during those spiritual attacks.

Thank You Lord, for leading me into Your arms.
Thank You Lord, for with You I am back.
So humbled and grateful am I,
for in You, there is nothing I lack.

My Journey With The Rosary

As I hold the rosary in my hands,
I feel its beads and the gentle weight.
Each one reminds me of a prayer,
a moment to pause and connect with God.

I start with the cross, whispering my faith,
inviting Jesus into my heart.
With every Hail Mary, I find calm,
my worries fade, and peace settles in.

In the Joyful Mysteries, I reflect,
the Annunciation, when hope was born.
Mary's visit to Elizabeth brings joy,
and the Nativity fills my heart with love.

I see the Presentation in the Temple,
when Simeon held the promise of God.
The Finding of Jesus in the Temple,
reminds me to seek Him in my life.

The Sorrowful Mysteries draw me near,
the Agony in the Garden brings tears.
I feel His pain as He takes my sins,
and the Scourging at the Pillar breaks my heart.

I witness His crown of thorns, heavy and cruel,
and the journey to Calvary weighs on my soul.
In His Crucifixion, I see His love,
and in His death, I find my hope.

In the Glorious mysteries, I rejoice,
the Resurrection brings me new life.
The Ascension lifts my spirit high,
as He promises to be with me always.

The Assumption of the Blessed Virgin Mary,
her body and soul taken to heaven,
fills me with hope for life beyond,
a reminder of the love that never ends.

The Coronation of the Blessed Virgin Mary,
reminds me of her love and grace for me.
As she reigns in glory, I find peace,
knowing she intercedes for me with tenderness.

In the Luminous Mysteries, I walk with Him,
the Baptism in Jordan opens my heart.
The Wedding at Cana shows His care,
transforming water into joy and life.

The Proclamation of the Kingdom calls me,
to live in love and share the Good News.
The Transfiguration lifts my soul to see,

His glory shining bright before my eyes.

The Institution of the Eucharist feeds my spirit,
reminding me of His love in every meal.
As I finish each decade, I feel renewed,
my heart grateful for the journey.

The rosary becomes my guiding path,
leading me closer to God every day.
With every prayer, I grow in faith,
learning to trust and surrender my fears.

In the quiet moments, I find strength,
In the stillness, my heart takes flight,
as prayers lift me towards the endless light,
knowing that I am never alone on this journey.

A Sanctuary Of Christ's Peace

As I enter the sacred space,
the familiar scent of incense fills the air,
I find my heart quieting,
preparing to meet the Lord in the Mass.

In the gathering of faithful souls,
I feel the warmth of community,
each face a reminder of His love,
each voice lifting prayers to the heavens.

The readings echo in my mind,
God's words touching the depths of my heart,
calling me to reflect, to repent,
to seek His peace in the midst of chaos.

When the priest lifts the Bread and Wine,
I am drawn into the mystery of grace,
the transformation before my eyes,
the gift of Christ's Body and Blood.

In this moment of Holy Communion,
I feel the weight of my burdens lift,
His peace washing over me,
calming the storms within my soul.

As I share the Sign of Peace,
I extend my hand, my heart, my love,
connecting with others in His name,
reminding us that we are all one Body.

In the Eucharistic prayer,
I listen as heaven and earth unite,
the angels singing in joyful praise,
and I join their chorus with gratitude.

In receiving the Blessed Sacrament,
I become one with Him, the source of peace,
the gentle whisper of His presence,
guiding me through my daily struggles.

As I leave the church, I carry His light,
the peace of Christ shining within me,
a beacon of hope for the world outside,
inviting others to find Him in their hearts.

In the quiet moments that follow,
I reflect on the grace bestowed,
knowing that I am never alone,
for His peace walks beside me always.

When Anxious

Today Lord, I kneel at Your feet,
in humility and surrounded with defeat.
My problems all crush me down,
I neither can get up nor lie down.
I know Lord that You have the greatest plans for
me,
but from where I stand, I just cannot see.
I know Lord that all I have to do is trust You
and that, I am trying to do.
But still, my eyes never cease to be filled
and my throat gets so parched.
The heaviness of my heart just refuses to go away
even when I know that You are my only way.
Every morning I pray that maybe this is the day
to receive the miracle for which I pray.
A small one, Lord, is all I ask for today
to keep me going all through the day.
Did You give it to me or did I fail to see
the miracle You have for me?
Lord, I feel so forsaken today,
so broken, alone and I do not know how to pray.
Please, Lord, be real when my faith fails me.
All I want is a touch or a hug consoling me
to know for sure that You are near me.
But I need You to be real in front of me.

I am very tired, Lord, and I cannot go on.
Please do not hide from me
and please show Your assuring self to me.

O Merciful Hour (The Hour That Jesus Died)

O Merciful Hour, please be still
so I can immerse in the Ocean of Mercy.
I want to drench in the Precious Blood.
Please be still; please do not pass by,
so my tears can be shed, not once
but many times over and over again.
Yet guilty; still, I would be for I nailed
my Saviour to the Cross.

The burden of my sins my Lord bore.
For every sin, the lashing I can hear.
The tightening of thorns suffocates my heart.
The thundering thud of the hammer,
my sins they make me remember,
and the tearing of Your flesh cringes me.
Let me hold to the cross so tightly
if it gives me that little repose to my disturbed
soul.

O Merciful Hour, what can soothe my soul?
What can loosen the suffocating grip on my heart?
What can strengthen my weakened knees
or give comfort to my teary eyes?

If You have to pass for Glory, then let it be,
for Your death will not be the end,
but the beginning of our story
of a new life in You, our Risen Lord.

In The Silence Of Suffering

In the quiet of night, when shadows creep,
I feel the weight of illness, a burden so deep.
My body aches, a reminder of my plight,
yet in this darkness, I seek Your light.
O Jesus, my healer, my comfort, my friend,
in You, I find strength; on You, I depend.
Each breath is a struggle, a fight to endure,
yet I cling to Your promise, steadfast and sure.
You walked among the weary, the lost and the
weak,
with hands that healed, hearts and solace You
seek.
I whisper my prayers, though my voice may be
faint.
In the depths of my pain, I find hope in Your
saints.
With every heartbeat, I am reminded of grace,
Your love wraps around me, a warm, sweet
embrace.
Though the road feels so heavy and nights seem so
long,
I hold onto Your words, my ever-true song.
In my moments of weakness, I hear Your soft call,
'Come, rest in My arms; I will carry it all'.
As my fever burns bright and my spirit feels low,

I envision Your face, and Your peace starts to flow.
In the depths of my suffering, I search for Your will,
for You know my journey, my heart You can fill.
O gentle Redeemer, in shadows I find,
a glimmer of hope that calms my troubled mind.
Through tears that fall freely, I still see Your grace.
Each drop is a prayer, a sacred embrace.
In the silence of suffering, Your presence is near.
With every heartbeat, I banish my fear.
You are my companion, my solace, my light,
guiding me gently through the long, lonely night.
So I rise from the darkness, my spirit renewed.
With faith as my armour, in love, I am imbued.
For even in sickness, I know I am blessed,
In Your hands, dear Jesus, I find my true rest.
I surrender my worries, my pain and my strife.
With You, O my Saviour, I embrace this new life.

Comfort In The Walk To Calvary

As I walk through my own trials,
I remember You, Lord, on that fateful path.
Each step heavy, a burden of sorrow,
You bore the weight of a world's pain.

Simon of Cyrene, compelled to help.
In my moments of struggle, I seek strength,
for I know that, like him, I can be a hand,
carrying the cross when I feel too weak.

The women of Jerusalem weep for You,
their tears mirror the love I feel in my heart.
Help me, Lord, to recognise those who grieve,
to offer comfort where sorrow resides.

And there was Veronica, brave and bold,
she stepped forward to wipe Your weary face.
In her act of love, I find my call,
to bring solace to those who bear heavy hearts.

Mary, Your mother, watching in anguish,
her love for You, a reflection of mine.
In my own struggles, I seek to stay close,

embracing the pain, the joy, the sacrifice.

John, the beloved, loyal to the end,
his presence, a reminder to stand by my friends.
May I be that source of steadfast support,
holding the light for those in the dark.

In my journey, Lord, I feel Your embrace,
each figure on Your path reminds me to love.
Help me to comfort, to carry, to share,
as I walk with You, finding strength in Your grace.

Embracing The Unknown

Lord, in the quiet hours of the night,
a fear creeps in, heavy and cold.
What lies beyond this life I know,
this fragile thread that holds me here?

I clutch the moments, each breath, each laugh,
fearing the silence that may come too soon.
Will I be forgotten, a whisper in the wind,
or will my love linger in the hearts I leave behind?

I tremble at the thought of letting go,
of leaving the warmth of familiar faces,
the comfort of laughter, the embrace of family.
Will I find my way in the dark unknown?

Lord, grant me peace in this uncertainty,
help me trust in Your promise of forever.
In the face of death, let me see life,
the beauty woven in every fleeting moment.

Teach me to live fully, to love fiercely,
to savour each blessing, each shared glance.
Let my heart be open, my spirit free,
to accept the journey, however it unfolds.

In You, I seek solace, a gentle light,
reminding me that love conquers all fears.
May I find hope in the promise of Your grace,
as I learn to embrace both life and its end.

Stepping Into The Unknown

When life leads me to deserts and wide seas,
I remember the Israelites, wandering, afraid,
no map, no landmarks, only the promise–
a land they could not yet see.
The Red Sea before them, towering waves,
yet they stepped forward,
feet touching the edge of uncertainty,
trusting God would part the waters.
I hold this in my heart
when the path ahead is nothing but questions,
when all I see are barriers looming.
Then, I recall the walls of Jericho,
fortress high and unbreakable.
Israelites circled them, in faith,
no weapons but a promise from God.
Day after day, they walked,
doubt close at their heels,
until the walls crumbled at His Word.
And so, I too walk around the walls in my life,
though they seem immovable,
trusting that God's timing will bring them down,
even if the way forward is still unclear.
And David, with nothing but a stone in hand,
stood before a giant, a wall of a man,
where fear would say to flee, he took aim.

One small act of faith, against all odds,
and God made the impossible fall.
When giants stand in my path,
and the tools I hold feel small,
I remember how God's strength shines
through simple, fragile steps,
and I take my own,
trusting that He will meet me there.
So, Lord, as I stand on the edge of the unknown,
give me courage to step where I cannot see.
Teach me to trust as the sea parts beneath my feet,
to wait as walls crumble in their time,
and to know that my smallest acts of faith
can bring down the giants I face.
When all around me is a question mark,
be my answer, my strength, my guide.
Lead me forward, step by step,
knowing You go before me in all things,
and in Your hands, I am safe.

At Heaven's Gate

It is finished. My journey is over.
Do not cry for me, for I am going to my Lord.
I leave behind the weight of this world,
but I take with me the love we shared.

There, at the gates, Jesus waits for me,
His arms open wide, His face full of light.
No fear remains; only peace fills my soul,
as I walk toward His gentle embrace.

Beside Him stands His Mother, so tender,
with eyes that have known every sorrow.
She greets me like her own, pulling me close,
and I feel her love surround me whole.

All the angels gather in songs of welcome,
a chorus of grace I had only dreamt of.
They lift me higher, beyond pain and time,
into a joy that knows no end.

And there, among saints, I had prayed to,
the faithful who walked this path before,
I see familiar faces shining bright–
my loved ones, waiting, their smiles pure.

Do not grieve, for I am not lost.
I have found my true home, my resting place.
In this realm of love and endless light,
I am free, at peace and fully alive.

So remember me, not with sorrow,
but with a quiet faith that sees beyond.
I am with you still, in spirit and grace,
held forever in the heart of God.

Guided Through The Mist

I do not know what lies ahead of me.
The mist is dark but not at all dreary.
My next step I do not know,
but I refuse to stay low.
My spirit is not confined,
and calmness fills my mind,
because I know that I am not alone
in the future unknown.
For Jesus is there with me,
whatever my situation be.
The road ahead does not frighten me,
for He, my strength, will always be.
He will scoop me from every bad happening,
and make me soar on eagle's wings.
Without Him, my life has no meaning,
for He is the essence of my every being.
Jesus, you are my God, my Saviour and King,
in your love, I find my heart's true spring.
Though the mist may hide what's ahead,
I trust in the path you have laid and led.
Your hand guides me through each unknown,
in your grace, I will never be alone.
Through every shadow, your light will shine,
for I am Yours, and You are mine.
So, I will step forward without a fear,

for I know Your presence is always near.
My Saviour, my King, my heart's only song,
with You, my journey is where I belong.

My Guardian And Guide

O my angel, my guardian and guide,
be with me in every stride.
Through morning light and darkest night,
stay close; keep me within your sight.

You who know my fears and dreams,
each silent prayer, each whispered plea,
walk beside me through unseen paths.
Steady my steps, set my spirit free.

In moments of doubt when shadows fall,
let your gentle light break through.
With wings of mercy, lift me high,
and remind me I am safe with you.

O faithful friend, unseen yet near,
you guard me with a love so pure.
In joy and sorrow, peace and pain,
your presence helps me to endure.

When I falter, lost and afraid,
whisper hope into my heart.
Guide me back to where I belong,
with strength and courage to restart.

Teach me to listen; teach me to see
the path that leads to God's embrace.
And through each trial, stay by my side,
my angel, my shield, my gift of grace.

So here I walk, not alone, but known,
held in hands both gentle and wise.
O my angel, my guardian and guide,
in every step, with you, I rise.

Beyond The Daily Grind

In the blur of days that roll, unkind,
we chase each task, leave peace behind.
The hours are swift, yet burdens slow.
Each challenge faced, our spirits know.

When duties stack, like stones they weigh,
and tempers fray along the way.
What joy can come from toil's embrace?
In God alone, we find our place.

The weight of words, misunderstood,
we aim to build but splintered wood.
Through every step, a trial to face,
and fleeting are our gifts of grace.

In whispered prayers, we seek the light,
to guide us through each restless night.
Yet walls arise, tall, firm and strong–
in faith, we find where we belong.

We strive for more, yet still we lack,
the load grows heavy on our backs.
Ambitions falter, dreams grow faint,
in shadows, doubts begin their taint.

Yet in this struggle, there's a peace,
a gentle call bids worries cease.
Our fleeting goals may come and go,
but God's embrace remains our glow.

So when the weary road seems long,
and things go right but feel all wrong,
we lift our gaze beyond this earth,
to Him who gave our spirits birth.

In every trial, His strength we claim,
through joy or pain, we praise His name.
In work's embrace, may He be found,
our steadfast Rock, our Holy Ground.

Finding You From Dawn To Rest

Lord, in the morning light I rise,
to find You here, to my surprise.
In quiet dawn, as the day begins,
I feel Your love, where life begins.
With each small task from room to room,
in breakfast made and beds resumed,
let me be mindful; see Your face,
within each moment, find Your grace.
Through sweeping floors and setting right,
in laundry folded, washed to white,
I pray to find Your presence near,
in every task, Your voice I hear.
When midday comes, in pause and meal,
let gratitude and peace reveal
the sacred rhythm of each hour,
the gentle flow of love's pure power.
In errands run and needs attended,
help me to see each day extended
as a gift from You, where I am blessed
to serve with joy, to know Your rest.
As evening falls, in table spread,
I gather close those I am led
to love and cherish, hearts in tune,

while night's soft quiet comes so soon.
In nightly prayers, as lamps grow dim,
I lift my thanks, my hope in Him.
Till sleep enfolds and dreams abide,
I know You walk here by my side.
From dawn till night, till rest is near,
Your presence, Lord, is ever clear.
In all I do, my heart shall see–
You dwell here, Lord, in love with me.

Be With Me, Lord

I am embarking on a journey–
will You be with me, Lord?
With each uncertain step I take,
guide me, hold me close to Your Word.

Be with those who are taking me there,
keep them steady, safe and wise.
Let Your love surround their hearts,
and bring peace where fear might rise.

Be with my fellow travellers, too,
those I meet along the way.
In moments shared and paths crossed,
help us find You in each day.

Through unknown roads and winding trails,
be my compass, true and clear.
In every valley, over every hill,
let me feel that You are near.

Give me courage when I am weak,
patience when I long to stray.
Teach me to trust with each new mile,
and faith to face another day.

So here I am, Lord, ready to go,
knowing You are my steady light.
Through every moment, come what may,
stay with me, in peace and might.

At The Crossroads

Lord, today I am standing at crossroads,
do not know which way to go, what decision to take.
With roads diverging and shadows that load,
a heart that trembles, a path yet to make.

Your whispers are faint, yet call me to trust,
in the silence where my fears collide.
Each choice a question, each turn a gust,
as doubt and faith walk side by side.

The road to the left seems rugged and steep.
Its stones like trials, its hills unknown.
But in each step, perhaps treasures to keep,
lessons to learn and seeds to be sown.

The path to the right glows soft and wide.
Yet shadows lurk in the light I see.
Will I lose myself in its comfort's tide,
or find what You have truly meant for me?

I stand here still, in my humble plea,
waiting, watching for Your guiding light.
Lord, breathe Your wisdom deep into me,
to see which way my soul finds right.

What if the path I choose is a test,
a refining fire, a season of pain?
Will I trust Your promise to give me rest,
or falter beneath the weight of the strain?

Lord, teach me to see not just the roads,
but the journey itself as a gift of grace.
With You as my guide, I will bear my loads,
and find in the struggle Your holy embrace.

So here I wait, not alone but with grace,
where roads converge beneath heaven's dome.
In You, my God, I find my place,
wherever I go, You are my home.

The Divine Mercy In My Life

At three o'clock, the world pauses,
as the hour of mercy calls my heart to stillness.
I remember Your passion, Lord, the agony and
love,
in this sacred moment, I draw near to You.

I close my eyes and the weight of my burdens
softens in the warmth of Your compassion.
With each tick of the clock, I surrender my fears,
trusting in Your promise; Your mercy abounds.

In my heart, I echo St. Faustina's prayer,
'Jesus, I trust in You', a lifeline for my soul.
At this hour, I feel Your love wash over me,
a river of grace, making me whole.

When my doubts arise and shadows creep in,
I seek refuge in this divine embrace.
The wounds of Your heart pour forth healing,
filling my spirit with courage and grace.

Lord, in this moment, I lift my intentions,
for those who suffer, for those who despair.
May they feel Your mercy, a soothing balm,
hope to the hopeless, a reminder You care.

As I reflect on Your passion, I am renewed,
Your sacrifice reminds me of love's true cost.
At three o'clock, I pause, my heart open wide,
receiving the mercy that conquers all loss.

Help me to carry this grace into my days,
to be a vessel of mercy, reflecting Your light.
In every encounter, may I share Your love,
for in Your Divine Mercy, I find my true sight.

Morning Whispers Of Prayer

In the hush of the night, while the world sleeps,
I wake up; my Lord I seek.
In silence, my heart in reverence invokes,
the mighty Lord, my Saviour, I cloak.

As the first light of the day dances softly on the walls,
a gentle reminder of the grace that befalls.
My heart pours out all its praises,
with eyes closed tight, I whisper my dreams.

In this moment holy, my spirit redeems.
With each line of prayer, my soul refreshed,
in the moment of divineness, my faith is restored.
In the moment of stillness, I pray to my Lord.

With the soft winds that brush against my face,
I sense Your presence, Your comforting embrace.
No words can capture this peace so profound;
in Your love, my fears are drowned.

Each whispered plea, a step closer to You,
guiding my heart with mercies new.
The day ahead may bring trials to face,
but I rise, shielded by Your grace.

No matter what comes, I am not alone,
for You are my refuge, my eternal home.
Morning whispers, as soft as a dove,
carry my prayers to the heavens above.

And as the sun rises, warming the sky,
I feel Your presence, always nearby.
I carry Your peace into the day's start;
with You, my Lord, forever in my heart.

In The Smallest Of Things

I see You, Lord, in the smallest of things–
a glimmer of light through leaves at dawn,
the quiet drift of a single feather,
a flower's face turning toward the sun.

In the gentle curve of a child's hand,
the soft breath of wind that brushes my cheek,
the glistening dew that clings to grass–
there, too, is Your presence, tender and near.

You hide in the humble, the overlooked,
in the smallest gifts, unseen by most.
Yet my heart feels Your touch in all these things,
and I know You are here, always and close.

Teach me to seek You, not in grandeur,
but in whispers, the unnoticed grace–
to find Your love in the quiet moments,
and see Your face in the smallest of things.

Finding God's Presence In The Psalms

In the quiet of my heart,
I open the Psalms,
each word speaks to me,
inviting me into God's presence,
where my worries fade away,
and my spirit feels light.

When I feel lost and alone,
I read about David's fears,
his cries echo my own,
reminding me I am not abandoned,
for God is my refuge and strength,
a safe place in the storms of life.

In times of despair,
I find comfort in His words,
'Do not be afraid; I am with You',
ringing true in my heart,
lifting me from my sadness,
filling me with hope once more.

When joy fills my heart,
I sing with the psalmist in praise,

celebrating the blessings I have,
lifting my hands in thanks,
for each new day that dawns,
for every breath that I take.

In dark valleys,
I cling to His light,
His rod and staff, my comfort,
reminding me I am not alone,
for in my weakness, He is strong,
His presence gives me strength.

I think of His goodness,
the love that lasts forever,
I see His hand in nature,
in the beauty all around,
the rustling leaves, the flowing streams,
whispering how much He cares.

In quiet moments,
I hear Him speak through the verses,
each line brings peace to my soul,
reminding me to be still and know,
that He is God, always near,
woven into my daily life.

When doubts fill my mind,
I turn to the Psalms for help,

finding peace in His faithfulness,
a reminder that I am loved,
His love never ends,
a source of grace in my journey.

In my prayers, I share my heart,
the psalms guiding my words,
teaching me to express my pain,
my hopes, my dreams, my fears,
knowing He hears each cry,
and answers with love.

As I move through each day,
I carry the Psalms in my heart,
their wisdom shaping my thoughts,
my actions, my desires,
a reminder of His constant presence,
my guide through life's challenges.

In every season, I find Him there,
in the highs and lows, in the simple moments,
each day a chance to connect,
to feel His love and mercy,
for He is my refuge, my song, my God.

Alleluia, Your Creation Praise

The sun breaks out into a brilliant shine from a restful hue,
the mountains send forth their streams of music.
The birds perched on the trees sing their songs in varied notes,
while the choir in the church raises their voices to Alleluia.

Alleluia, my Lord, Your creation praises You for all that You have done.
Alleluia, my Lord, we declare You are our God.
Alleluia, my Lord, there is no other God like You,
so majestic, clothed in splendour and overflowing in love.

The oceans clap their waves against the shore,
the trees sway in rhythm; their branches adore.
The stars at night twinkle in their place,
each one reflecting a glimpse of Your grace.

The wind whispers Your name through the fields of grain,
while the rain dances down, singing its refrain.
The flowers bloom, their petals unfold,
declaring Your beauty, more precious than gold.

Alleluia, my Lord, the heavens declare Your power.
Alleluia, my Lord, in every sunrise, You shower
Your mercy, Your grace, with each new dawn,
and in Your light, we are forever drawn.

The earth sings, the skies proclaim,
all of creation glorifies Your name.
And as we join the chorus in praise,
our hearts lift high, our voices raise.

Alleluia, my Lord, from every corner of the Earth,
we sing Your praise, acknowledging Your worth.
Alleluia, my Lord, forever we will sing,
Your creation, Your people; to You we cling.

The Night Of Salvation

In the twilight sky,
the star shone so bright.
A cold night and all asleep,
yet the shepherds watched their sheep.

It was a night that the prophets foretold;
it was a night that every year its story is told;
it was a night we will always behold;
when the story of salvation started to unfold.

Salvation was born that night,
and very few were witnesses to that sight.
A King was born, not in splendour,
yet worshipped in all grandeur.

The wonder of that night
still fills our souls with delight
and stirs the air with a magical peace
that makes our hearts be at ease.

Angels sang with voices so high,
Glory to God, they cried to the sky.
The heavens rejoiced at this humble birth,
as love descended to grace the Earth.

In a manger, the Saviour laid His head.
Where animals slept, He found His bed.
Yet even there, His light shone true,
a promise of hope for me and you.

The silence of that holy night,
was filled with awe and heaven's light.
For in that moment, so meek and small,
came the greatest gift given to all.

And now we sing that ancient song,
for the night of salvation still lives on.
In our hearts, His love we hold,
a story forever to be told.

In Praise Of Ave Maria

In silence, I hear the gentle call,
a whisper of grace, my sweetest thrall.
'Ave Maria'; my heart begins to soar,
in the depths of my soul, I seek evermore.
O vessel of love, so pure and divine,
in your presence, dear Mary, my spirit will shine.
Gratia plena, the blessing you bear,
with each breath I take, I know you are there.
Through trials and sorrows, you lead me along,
in the darkest of nights, you are my song.
I lift up my voice in a humble refrain,
calling on you, Mary, to heal every pain.
In the warmth of your arms, I find my true peace,
with faith in your heart, my worries release.
O Mother of mercy, with eyes full of grace,
I feel your embrace in this sacred space.
Your love is a river, so deep and so wide,
with you by my side, I shall never divide.
You guide me through shadows; you light up my way,
in every moment, I kneel down and pray.
With fervent devotion, I carry your name,
in the whispers of prayers, I feel no shame.
Each Hail Mary spoken, is a step on my path,
I walk with your spirit, through joy and wrath.

In grace, I am lifted; my burdens grow light,
with you as my beacon, I stand in the light.
O sweet Ave Maria, my heart beats in time,
In the rhythm of faith, I rise, I climb.
So here I will linger, in love's gentle fold,
with stories of wonder and grace to be told.
Gratia plena, my song of the heart,
forever united, we shall never part.

The Beauty Of The Liturgy

In the stillness, as candles glow,
I find a peace that fills my soul.
Ancient words and chants arise,
lifting my spirit to the skies.

The incense rises, a fragrant prayer,
each breath a reminder – God is there.
I feel His presence, vast and near,
in every word, each song I hear.

The priest's voice rings, calm and sure,
a vessel of grace, steadfast and pure.
I am drawn to listen, heart laid bare,
as Scripture speaks, I meet Him there.

Bread and wine, both simple, true,
become His Body and Blood, made anew.
In this mystery, I am fed,
by Christ's own life, my daily bread.

The liturgy flows like a timeless stream,
bringing Heaven closer than it seems.
With every gesture, every word,
my heart is opened, my soul is stirred.

It fills my life with steady grace,
with sacred rhythm, holy pace.
Through feast and fast, joy and sorrow,
it shapes my path, today and tomorrow.

The Bells Of The Angelus

The bells ring out, calling my heart,
a holy summons through the morning light,
through noon's stillness, through dusk's calm–
their echo stirs my soul awake.

I pause, as heaven's memory unfolds:
the angel's greeting, humble and bold.
Hail Mary, full of grace, I breathe,
and in her 'Ye's, I feel my own.

The Word became flesh, dwelt among us–
mystery made real in love's pure gift.
I ask for her faith, her steadfast trust,
to open my heart, to make space within.

These bells, like whispers, draw me near,
to honour God's choice to be one with us.
May each chime shape my silent prayer,
an offering of love, simple and true.

Pray for me, Mother, as I pause in this hour,
to carry Christ's light into the world.

The 'I Am' In Me

You are the Bread that fills my soul,
when empty, lost, You make me whole.
On famished nights, You feed my needs,
in every word, my spirit's freed.

You are the Light that clears my way,
in shadowed paths, You turn night to day.
Your glow becomes my courage strong,
In You, I know where I belong.

You are the Gate that opens wide,
through You, I walk and fear subsides.
A Shepherd's gate to pastures true,
where peace and rest are found in You.

You are the Shepherd, kind and near,
in the darkest valleys, I feel no fear.
You know my name, You call me home,
with You beside me, I am never alone.

You are the Life; You conquer death,
in rising power, my soul finds rest.
The Resurrection lifts my gaze,
in You, I find unending days.

You are the Way, the Truth and Life,
through every storm, You are by my side.
In You, the path is clear and bright,
my compass true, my source of light.

You are the Vine where life flows free,
I cling to You; You grow in me.
With every breath, I feel Your grace–
in You, I find my dwelling place.

Mountains Of Glory, Valleys Of Faith

On Moriah's height, where faith is tested,
Abraham stands, his heart invested.
A knife raised high, yet mercy speaks–
a ram appears, the promise keeps.
Down below, the trials renew,
but here, we find our trust in You.

On Sinai's peak, where thunder rolls,
Moses receives Your law for souls.
With fire and cloud, Your voice commands,
writing truth upon stone for the land.
Below, the world is filled with strife,
yet here, You shape our way of life.

On Carmel's rise, Elijah prays,
your fire descends, a holy blaze.
False idols fall, Your truth revealed,
Your covenant in flame is sealed.
The valley calls with doubts and fears.
But strength is found in these tiers.

On Zion's hill, Jerusalem's throne,
a temple stands, Your sacred home.

A city sings, where worship flows,
and Your abiding presence grows.
Though life below may lose its song,
here, we see Your kingdom strong.

On Tabor's height, Your glory shone,
in robes of light, as Heaven's own.
With Moses, Elijah by Your side,
You strengthen us before the tide.
We descend with strength to bear,
our daily cross, with You in prayer.

On Calvary's slope, Your love laid bare,
the weight of sin, our burdens there.
The cross, the cries, the darkest sky–
our hope restored as You choose to die.
From this great height, Your mercy streams,
to heal our wounds and lift our dreams.

Lord, lead me up these heights again,
where strength is found and doubts grow thin.
In every valley, dark and wide,
reminds me of these peaks that guide.
For up these mountains, I draw near–
to live Your love and know You here.

Whispers In The Night

As darkness falls, I seek Your light,
in the shadows, I find my sight.
With every star that blinks in the sky,
I lift my heart with a sigh.

Lord, in this quiet hour,
I feel Your presence, a gentle power.
In silence, I whisper my hopes and fears,
trusting in love that calms my tears.

Bathe me in peace, like the moon's white glow,
wrap me in grace and let Your mercy flow.
Forgive my sins, both spoken and still,
grant me the strength to do Your will.

As the world rests, I pause and pray,
for loved ones near and those far away.
May angels guard through the silent night,
surrounding my soul with blessed light.

In gratitude, my blessings I count,
for each moment, Your love surrounds.
In trials faced, I find my way,
cause Your guidance leads me all the way.

So, as I lay down, my spirit in peace,
I trust in Your promise as my fears are released.
With every breath, I surrender my plight,
in faith, I find solace in You, my soul's delight.

Easter People

There He lay in the dark, all dead and forgotten.
What wrong had He begotten to be alone in death!
Just days ago, the crowd that shouted Alleluia,
was the same that roared, 'Crucify Him'! with hysteria.
His friends were filled with confusion and were scared,
perplexed at all that happened and at all that He had said.
Yet it was not to be that He lies in this state.
It was not to be that death would seal His fate.
In the wee hours of that morn,
a ray of hope from the cave was drawn,
and a glimmer of light through the shadows shone.
Growing to be a vortex of love,
drawing the hopeless to rise above.
Setting us free from all that we are not meant to be.
There He stands outside His tomb.
All in white and in splendour.
There he stands with His arms open wide.
His wounds still fresh on His palms, feet and His side.

He comes to His people so that we might believe,
that we, from our agony, be relieved.
He gave us the grace to be His Easter people,
to be all that He is – love.
To be boundless and free,
He gave us the grace to spread that love,
to everyone who is bound in fear and doubt.
So that they can break their chains and rise above,
free from their sins, their burdens cast out.

The Rosary – Her Strength

She passed the beads through her fingers,
her lips moving softly in whispered prayers.
Sometimes a pause, trying to remember
those sacred words taught in her younger years.
Each bead, her strength through life's trials and strife,
a lifeline to faith, as memory slips away.
I remember the way she taught me, too–
the same prayers she learned in her youth's bright days.
Daily prayers, a must as dusk approached,
her voice steady, even when it would falter,
instilling a faith that time could not erode,
her rosary, her anchor, unshaken, unaltered.
Though now her mind fades, piece by piece,
her fingers still trace the chain without cease.
In silence, she whispers a faith so profound;
even when lost, in prayer she is found.
I watch her now, the woman who held me near,
now fragile and distant, yet steadfast and true.
Her faith undiminished by passing years–
in those beads, her spirit remains anew.
Her hands once firm, now trembling and weak,
but in her gaze, there's strength that I seek.
A glimpse of the woman who shaped who I am,

teaching me faith like a cherished psalm.
Now, I hold her hand as she once held mine,
guiding her back to the words that shine.
In each bead, a history of love and grace,
a mother's gift that time cannot erase.
Though memory fades, the rosary stays,
a beacon of light through her wearied days.
And even as her thoughts may stray,
her faith is the constant that will not sway.

Ora Pro Nobis: Prayer For The Faithful

In moments heavy with doubt and despair,
I lift my heart, a silent prayer.
'Ora pro nobis', I softly plead,
for strength and guidance in every need.
So much to bear; the world weighs me down,
yet in my struggle, I will never drown.

The angels surround me; their wings spread wide,
with whispers of hope, they stand by my side.
Each saint a beacon, a light in the dark,
with faith like fire, they ignite my spark.
Their prayers ascend like incense sweet,
a chorus of love, where heaven and earth meet.

Mother Mary, with a heart so pure,
in your gentle presence, I find my cure.
You cradle my worries, my sorrows, my fears;
with tender compassion, you dry all my tears.
To Jesus, you carry my cries and my sighs;
in your motherly love, my spirit will rise.

When life's storms rage and I feel so small,
I cling to the promise, I will never fall.

For in this communion of saints and of grace,
I find my solace, my sacred space.
With each whispered prayer, my heart beats anew;
in this sacred journey, I will always be true.

So here I stand, in faith and in trust.
In the love of the Father, I find my must.
With angels and saints, and Mother so dear,
I know that in prayer, my heart will draw near.
'Ora pro nobis', I sing with delight;
in the embrace of their love, I find my light.

A Prayer For The Gift Of Life

Lord, we come with hearts that yearn,
for the blessing of life, for love to burn.
With open arms and humble hearts,
we wait on You, as life imparts.

In Your wisdom and perfect way,
we trust in Your timing, day by day.
For every moment, we are still,
learning to yield to Your holy will.

You know our dreams, our deepest prayer,
to welcome a child, our love to share.
Through this journey, please be near,
grant us patience; cast out fear.

When nights grow long and faith feels frail,
remind us, Lord, You will prevail.
In valleys low or mountains high,
help us believe, though we wonder why.

Give us strength when hope feels thin,
to trust Your plan, to hold within.
If it be Your will, let life begin,
a gift from You, our hearts akin.

We ask not only for our own,
but for each heart that feels alone.
Let every soul that seeks to be,
find comfort in Your sovereignty.

Bless us, Lord, with the joy of new light,
a child to cherish, a love made right.
In every laugh, in each small cry,
a glimpse of heaven, by and by.

For now, we wait with hands upturned,
in faith renewed, in hope unlearned.
Lord, hear our plea, our simple call,
and help us trust You, Lord of all.

A Prayer For Our Clergy

Lord, we lift our priests to You,
these humble men, both strong and true.
Chosen to serve, they give their all,
yet human still, they are prone to fall.

Grant them courage, steadfast grace,
in every step, in every place.
Guard their minds and guide their hands,
as they fulfil Your sacred plans.

For those who walk amidst the world,
whose hearts in earthly storms are swirled,
keep them pure, their spirits bright,
holding firm to truth and light.

For those in sickness, worn and weak,
who long to serve, who seek to speak–
in their frailty, be their might;
heal their souls, restore their sight.

For those grown frail with passing years,
whose strength is dimmed, whose sight unclear,
fill them with a holy fire,
the gentle flame of pure desire.

Though weary hands may shake and tremble,
still, they hold what none can measure–
the Bread and Wine of Life within their palm,
Your Body and Blood, Christ, their healing balm.

Bless them, Lord, with heaven's grace,
renew their hearts in every place.
Through joys and trials, dark and bright,
keep them always in Your light.

A Prayer For Caring For Aged Parents

Lord, I come to You with a humble heart,
seeking strength and patience for this journey.
As I care for my aged parents,
help me honour the lives they have lived.

Grant me the grace to see their wisdom,
in the stories shared, in the laughter remembered.
Help me listen deeply, with compassion,
to the fears that linger in their tired hearts.

In moments of frustration, remind me gently,
that they once held me close, nurtured my dreams.
Let my love flow freely, like a river,
offering comfort in their times of need.

Help me navigate the challenges we face,
to find joy in the small, everyday moments.
May I be their refuge, their safe space,
offering dignity in the twilight of life.

Guide my hands to serve with tenderness,
my words to uplift, to encourage, to soothe.

Let me cherish each fleeting moment,
as a gift, a blessing to be shared.

Lord, in caring for them, help me grow,
to learn the depths of love and sacrifice.
May our time together be filled with grace,
a beautiful dance of family and faith.

As they journey towards their final days,
may I be their light, their support, their joy.
Help me reflect Your love in every act,
for in serving them, I serve You, Lord.

A Prayerful Walk To Forever

Lord, as I walk this sacred path,
each step toward a life brand new,
my heart bows low in grateful awe,
for this love, this vow, this gift from You.

Grant me peace in every stride,
a steady heart, a soul at rest.
Prepare my spirit for this promise,
this covenant to love my best.

Teach me patience, grace and mercy,
to give as freely as You give,
to build a home where faith abides,
where kindness grows and hope can live.

In moments bright or shadowed dim,
be our guide, our bond, our light.
Join our hands and knit our hearts,
firmly held within Your sight.

Bless this union as I move
closer now, with trust in You.
In Your love, our strength will grow–
forever faithful, forever true.

A Prayer For Your Presence At Work

Lord Jesus, walk with me today,
in every task along the way.
In duties small, in duties great,
help me to serve and not to wait.

When plans go wrong and tempers flare,
when I feel lost or weighted with care,
remind me gently You are near,
my strength, my peace, my calm from fear.

When co-workers' words feel hard to bear,
and kindness seems beyond repair,
give me patience, grace and sight
to meet them, Lord, with love's own light.

In moments when confusion grows,
and deadlines press or worry shows,
steady my mind, renew my heart,
for in Your presence, fears depart.

When systems fail, when screens go black,
and tasks undone weigh on my back,
let me trust Your hand, Your way,

to guide me through each trying day.

Lord, fill my work with holy peace,
in every moment, let my joy increase.
May all I do reflect Your grace,
and find in You my resting place.

So as I toil from morn till end,
help me remember, Saviour and Friend,
that even in the smallest things,
Your love sustains; Your mercy sings.

A Prayer For A Contented Heart

Lord, calm my spirit, quiet my mind,
when I am quick to speak, let me pause and find
the blessings hidden in every day,
the peace that flows from words I pray.
Teach me to see what is good and bright,
to trust in You, my source of light.

When I am tempted to grumble or sigh,
and my soul feels weary, my spirit dry,
remind me gently of all You give–
the grace, the strength, the will to live.
Fill me with joy that cannot be shaken,
a heart in You, forever awakened.

In moments where gratitude seems far away,
help me to lean on You and stay
rooted deep in Your faithful love,
trusting in blessings from above.
Renew my heart to praise, not moan,
and know I am never here alone.

Lord, forgive the sighs and doubts,
transform my worries, cast them out.

Show me the beauty in trials and tears,
the faith that grows, dispelling fears.
Help me to see with humble eyes
Your hand at work, so wise.

Soften my heart with a grateful song,
teach me patience when things feel wrong.
When I am weak, make me strong in You,
content in all I say and do.
In trust, in peace, Lord, let me be
forever grateful, close to You.

A Prayer For Peace Amidst Pain

Lord, I come to You with a weary heart,
carrying aches that linger, fears that weigh.
In every anxious thought that stirs,
bring Your calm to guide my way.

When shadows of sickness cloud my mind,
and doubts begin to take their hold,
wrap me in Your healing light,
and let Your peace within unfold.

Grant me rest from worry's grip,
a release from fears that bind my soul.
Remind me, Lord, that through each trial,
Your gentle hand can make me whole.

Help me trust in Your steadfast care,
to find comfort in Your boundless grace.
Ease my spirit, soothe my pain,
and let me rest in Your embrace.

A Prayer To Release The Fear Of The Unknown

Lord, You know the depths of my heart,
the worries that creep in, the fears I cannot name.
In this vast unknown where I cannot see,
help me to find peace in Your guiding hand.

When I am faced with uncertainty,
and doubts cloud my path ahead,
grant me the strength to trust Your plan,
to walk in faith, not paralysed by fear.

Teach me to rest in Your promise, Lord,
to believe that You walk beside me always.
Though the future is hidden, beyond my sight,
Your love remains, steady and unchanging.

Take this burden of fear from my heart;
replace it with courage that comes from You.
Let me feel Your presence in every step,
and find joy in the journey, whatever may come.

Help me surrender each anxious thought,
to lean on You when I cannot see the way.
For You are my rock, my refuge, my light–

with You, Lord, there is nothing to fear.

Longing For The Beatitudes

In the stillness of my heart, I yearn,
for the wisdom in each word I learn.
'Blessed are the poor in spirit', I see,
in my weakness, I find humility.
The kingdom of heaven, a promise true,
in my brokenness, I am made anew.

'Blessed are those who mourn', I hear,
for comfort comes when I kneel and pray near.
Through tears of sorrow, I find His grace;
in every loss, I seek His face.
For joy will rise where pain once lay;
in mourning hearts, His love will stay.

'Blessed are the meek', the gentle call;
in their quiet strength, I see the thrall.
I long to let go of pride's fierce grasp,
to offer love, a tender clasp.
In meekness, I will learn to stand tall;
in patience and peace, I will answer the call.

'Blessed are those who hunger and thirst
for righteousness', my soul will burst.
To seek the truth, to crave the right;
in every struggle, I will find the light.

With passion ignited, I will fight for the just;
in my heart and spirit, I place my trust.

'Blessed are the merciful', I strive to be,
to offer compassion, to set hearts free.
In every kindness, I see His face;
in acts of love, I find my place.
With open hands and a gentle heart,
in mercy's embrace, we will never part.

'Blessed are the pure in heart', I sigh,
to see the world through heaven's eye.
I strive to cleanse my thoughts and deeds,
to plant in others the love that feeds.
In purity, I will find my way,
to walk in truth, come what may.

'Blessed are the peacemakers', I aspire,
to calm the storms, to fan the fire.
With gentle words and open hands,
I long to build where love expands.
In every conflict, I will seek to mend;
in every heart, I will be a friend.

'Blessed are those who are persecuted for the sake
of right';
in trials faced, I seek His light.
For theirs is the kingdom, a promise divine;

in every struggle, His love will shine.
Though I may stumble, I will rise again
to walk in faith, my closest friend.

With each beatitude, a path unfolds,
a journey marked with truths of old.
In following Him, my spirit swells;
in living love, my heart compels.
In every blessing, I find my way,
longing for His light, come what may.

As I Come To Receive You

Lord, as I walk down this holy aisle,
my heart beats faster, drawn toward You.
Each step feels like a lifetime of waiting,
a longing I can barely contain.
I come with hands open, empty yet full,
my spirit trembling in Your presence.
This Bread and Wine this mystery,
beyond my knowing – yet I believe, I trust, I reach.

You call me forward, unworthy as I am,
clothed in Your mercy, wrapped in Your love.
I bring all that I am, my flaws and my fears,
my joys and my deepest regrets.
At this moment, nothing else matters,
for I stand before You, wholly known.
You look past my failures, my doubts, my pride;
You see only my yearning to be Yours.

As I near You, I feel the weight of Your love,
a love that gave everything to me.
You became flesh, entered my world,
took on my sorrows, carried my sins.
In this Holy Sacrament, You are here, real and present,

waiting to enter my soul.
I am overcome, humbled, in awe–
how could You choose to dwell in one like me?

But still, You invite me, saying,
'Come'. In this Bread and Wine, You are life itself.
I lift my hands, my heart, my very soul,
praying You fill every empty space.
Let Your presence be my strength,
Your peace my refuge; Your love my light.
As I receive You, Lord, let me become more like
You,
transformed by Your grace.

With each taste of this Sacred Mystery,
I surrender all I am and hope to be.
In You, I am whole, healed, forgiven; in You,
I am loved beyond measure.
Lord, as I walk away from this moment,
stay with me; guide my every step.
May I carry You within, a living tabernacle,
bearing Your love to all I meet.

In The Quiet Of Confession

Lord Jesus, I come, heavy with faults,
my heart weighed down, aching for mercy.
You know each hidden corner of my soul,
the flaws I hide, the sins I fear to name.

In this silence, I stand before You,
my words stumble, unworthy yet hopeful.
Teach me, Lord, how to be honest,
how to let go of all that binds me.

I bring You the pride that blinds my heart,
the anger I hold, fierce and silent.
The selfishness I cling to, wrapped tight,
my failures to love, the times I turned away.

You see the moments I withheld kindness,
the harsh words spoken out of my pain.
The hurt I caused, left unattended–
Lord, lift this weight; teach me to heal.

Here, in Your presence, my faults laid bare,
I feel the piercing light of Your love.
It searches, it cleanses, it renews,
calling me back to life, to grace.

Help me, Lord, to begin anew,
to walk again with courage and hope.
In Your mercy, I find my strength;
in Your forgiveness, I find my peace.

Guide me to live in truth and compassion,
to seek You in each step, each choice.
Let this confession be my turning,
my heart reborn, held close by You.

A Plea For Your Presence

A plea for Your presence, O Saviour, so near,
in this world of sorrow, I long for You here.
The burdens I carry, too heavy to bear,
I seek Your compassion, Your tender care.
Through trials and storms, through valleys so deep,
I call to You, Jesus, my soul longs to keep.
The noise of this world drowns out Your sweet voice,
yet in You, my heart finds peace and rejoice.
A thirst for Your presence, I cannot deny.
O Lord, come quickly, my soul cannot lie.
Your grace, like a river, flows deep in my soul,
It heals every wound, it makes me whole.
I search for Your guidance, I seek Your light,
to lead me through darkness, to make all things right.
When shadows surround me and hope fades away,
Your presence, O Saviour, will brighten my day.
In moments of weakness, when I feel so small,
I reach out to You, my Saviour, my all.
Your love is unchanging, Your mercy is true,
my heart is uplifted, O Lord, only You.
A plea for Your presence, my heart's deepest cry,
to walk in Your steps, to soar and to fly.

In the quiet of morning, or the still of the night,
I yearn for Your presence to make all things right.
So come, gentle Savior, be with me, I pray,
stay close to my heart, don't turn me away.
A plea for Your presence, O Christ, I implore,
fill me with Your Spirit, forevermore.

Jesus, You Are Too Slow

Jesus, You are too slow,
but You are perfect in Your timings.
Jesus, I am too hasty,
and my timings are all wrong.

It may seem that this is the moment to let things happen,
but You just do not budge an inch to let it happen.
You just smile and say, 'In My time'.
I may holler and cry to get my way through,
but You only gently chide, 'It is not My time'.

I may stomp the ground to make You do my way,
but You only nod and say, 'No way'.
The one thing I have learned in all the haste
is to just sit at Your feet
and let things happen in Your way, in Your pace.

In the silence, I hear Your whisper,
'Patience, dear child, I am right here'.
With every moment that feels like a test,
You remind me that waiting is part of the quest.

When my heart races and doubts creep in,

You offer me peace that flows from within.
In the stillness, Your presence I find,
A gentle reminder to rest my mind.

I learned that in waiting, there is strength to be found.
In trusting Your plan, my feet are on solid ground.
Though I may wish for a quicker reply,
I see that in Your timing, my spirit can fly.

So I will embrace this journey, however long,
for I know with You, I will always belong.
Each moment I linger in this holy space,
and I am learning to cherish Your infinite grace.

Jesus, You are too slow,
but in Your patience, I finally know,
that every delay is a chance to grow,
in love and in faith, I will let my heart show.

O Blessed Sacrament

I will have only You, Lord,
for only You satisfy my soul.
In my longing, I find no peace
until I rest in Your control.
My whole being aches for You,
the joy only Your presence brings;
nothing compares to this holy grace,
where my spirit sighs and sings.
Everything else becomes irrelevant
when I am enfolded in Your light.
In this quiet, sacred stillness,
You turn my darkness into sight.
Only You and I, that is it and no one else,
only You, O Blessed Sacrament–
My heart leans close, my soul surrenders,
as I bask in Your holy scent.
No one can do what You did for me,
suffered, bled and died alone;
for love beyond all telling,
You made my heart Your home.
O my soul's delight, let me receive You
in the Sacrament, holy and pure–
this is my Heaven here on Earth,
in Your love, so deep and sure.
What can I offer You, my King,

when I am so small and You so grand?
All I can give is my poor heart,
to hold in Your gentle hand.
Stay close to me, dwell in my soul,
and never let me fall away.
Let Your fire fill my hollow places,
and be my strength each day.
O Blessed Sacrament, Fount of mercy,
a well of love poured out for me,
I thirst for You, my soul's own rest,
in Your presence, bound and free.
Only You can quench my hunger,
only You can soothe my pain;
My life is Yours, my Saviour dear,
in the silence, Your peace remains.
In the quiet, I hear Your voice so clear,
like a whisper, soft and true.
You call my name, and I am drawn
to give my heart anew.
Here in Your love, time fades away,
and all my burdens cease;
Nothing I seek but You, my Lord–
in Your presence, I find peace.
No treasures of this world compare
to the sweetness I find in prayer;
Your love is light upon my path,
Your grace, a balm to every care.
Draw me closer, keep me near,

until I am wholly one with You.
O Blessed Sacrament, heart of my heart,
in Your love, my soul is free.

The Hem Of Your Garment

Let me touch the hem of Your garment,
and my mind will be at peace, I know.
In the quiet hush of mercy's sound,
where only You and I can go.
My weary thoughts laid gently down,
resting where Your grace will flow.

Let me touch the hem of Your garment,
to find healing where I hurt the most.
In doubts and fears that weigh me down,
where I have felt like a wandering ghost.
Only You can lift this heavy crown,
For in Your love, I am engrossed.

Let me touch the hem of Your garment,
when life's burdens press so near.
In every stumble, fall and frown,
You draw close and calm my fear.
In Your presence, I will drown,
and feel Your mercy, crystal-clear.

Let me touch the hem of Your garment,
with hands that tremble, heart laid bare.
To be lifted, even broken down,
and know that You are truly there.

In that touch, my soul is found,
my faith renewed beyond measure.

Healer Of My Soul

I came to You, broken, worn by pain,
a leper cast aside, left to wither alone.
But Your hand reached through my isolation,
touching me whole, restoring my flesh and soul.

Blindness bound me, darkness my only sight,
no colours, no faces, just shadows and night.
Yet You placed mud upon my eyes,
and light burst forth; I saw the world anew.

My legs, twisted and weak, lay lifeless, still.
I could only watch as others walked by.
Then Your voice called me to rise and stand,
and strength surged through, lifting me high.

I was lost in chains, my mind torn apart,
demon-driven, with no place to rest.
Yet You commanded, peace returned,
and calm settled deep within my chest.

Twelve years, my life drained away unseen,
a flow that would not cease, a wound unseen.
But I touched the hem of Your garment's grace,
and healing flowed – Your power released.

Now I know You, not just as healer and friend,
but as the One who sees the wounds, none can mend.
With each touch, each word, You bring me near,
and I walk whole, held in love without end.

My Victory Is Yours

I have finally accomplished, with You, my Lord,
for You are my strength, my unshaken ground.
In each step, each trial, You carried me,
and now I stand where hope and grace abound.

Through storms that raged and nights that
loomed,
You were my shelter, steady and sure.
When I faltered, You lifted me high,
until my spirit could endure.

Every struggle, each burden I bore,
You lightened with love, deep and pure.
In weakness, I leaned into Your power,
finding in You the will to endure.

Now I see the path we travelled together,
the valleys crossed, the mountains climbed.
With each hard-won mile, You led me on,
and my soul's song now rings in time.

This victory I call my own is Yours,
for in Your grace, I found my fight.
It's Your strength that filled my heart,
and brought me through the darkest night.

So here I stand, grateful and free,
with open hands and spirit bowed.
My triumph rests in Your loving arms,
my Saviour, my strength, my God.

Grace To Forgive

Lord, give me the grace to let go,
to forgive those who have wounded me deeply.
I release their hold on my heart,
every burden they have left within me.
I lay down the weight of each memory,
each hurt and hand them into Your care.
Keep them well, Lord, for they too are Yours,
guided by Your mercy, shaped by Your love.
But, oh Lord, how hard it is to forget,
when the scars still whisper their pain.
The echoes of words, the sting of betrayal,
linger like shadows that I cannot outrun.
Teach me, Lord, to see beyond myself,
to remember that Your love covered all sin,
even mine, even theirs.
Let me lean not on my strength but on Yours,
for alone, I falter, and bitterness consumes.
Let my spirit be free of resentment,
washed clean of bitterness and pain.
Teach me to see them as You do,
with compassion that stretches beyond my reach.
I ask only this, that Your grace remains with me,
steady as breath, close as my soul.
Do not take Your kindness from me, Lord;
let it flow like healing through each wound.

Help me, Lord, to unclench these fists,
to let go of the need for justice on my terms.
Remind me that vengeance is Yours, not mine,
and that Your justice is perfect, Your timing divine.
Fill the void left by hurt with Your presence,
a balm that soothes, a love that heals.
Teach me to walk in forgiveness, not just once,
but daily, as often as needed, with every step.
Where there was anger, plant Your peace;
where hurt has lingered, sow forgiveness.
Shape my heart in gentleness,
softened by Your endless mercy.
Draw me nearer to You, free from the chains of resentment,
open to love again.
Let me walk in the light of Your grace,
renewed by the courage to forgive.
Lord, as I forgive, forgive me too,
for holding on too tightly, for nursing my pain.
May my heart reflect Yours,
a wellspring of mercy, a sanctuary of peace.
For in forgiving, I am set free,
to live, to love and to be Yours completely.

A Mother's Longing

Will I ever be able to conceive?
Will I hold a baby, feel the weight,
of tiny hands that curl in mine,
of a heartbeat, I did not create?

I have kept this longing, quiet, deep.
A prayer woven through my soul.
Each passing month, a silent grief,
an empty cradle, an unfilled role.

I imagine whispers in the night,
Soft breaths, the warmth of skin on skin.
I hold that vision close to me,
Wondering if it is ever meant to begin.

I watch others with their little ones,
their laughter light, their joy so full.
And I wonder why my arms stay bare,
why my heart endures this aching pull?

Some nights I lie awake and dream
of a child who looks like me somehow,
With eyes so new, with hands that reach–
I can almost feel that moment now.

But days go on, and silence stays;
I bear this quiet ache alone.
A mother's heart, without a child,
a love unseen, a seed unsown.

If my path is not to bring life forth,
to feel that weight within my arms,
then, Lord, grant peace to my wounded soul,
and shield it gently from these storms.

For even dreams can break a heart,
and hope can cut as sharp as a loss.
Yet still I hold, with fragile strength,
this mother's love, no matter the cost.

A Prayer For The Souls In Purgatory

O Merciful Father, source of all light,
I come before You in the stillness of night.
With a heart open wide, I lift up in prayer
those souls in waiting, held within Your care.

For those we have loved, now veiled from sight,
grant them peace; embrace them with light.
In purgatory's depths, where sorrows cease,
pour forth Your mercy; bring them release.

Remember, O Lord, those we have left behind–
forgotten souls, hidden from the mind.
Shine on them, Lord, Your boundless grace,
and hasten them to Your holy embrace.

For the souls of strangers, for friends we hold
dear,
through our prayers, draw them near.
Lift the veil, remove the stain,
of sins now cleansed in purgatory's pain.

O Lamb of God, once sacrificed,
cleanse them in love, O Living Christ.

Let not one soul be left alone,
without the warmth of Your heavenly throne.

Father, in Your mercy, hear our plea;
grant them peace; let them be free.
May our love, our prayers, ease their way,
and guide them to Your eternal day.

For every soul, known and unknown,
we trust in Your mercy, which ever has shone.
Bring them, O Lord, to their heavenly rest,
in the light of Your love, eternally blessed.

Blessed Are The Shepherds

Blessed are the priests for their consecrated life,
a sacrificial life overpowering in His grace.
Blessed are they, the pleasing fragrance of Christ,
spreading His love through all His people.

Blessed are they, set apart only for His Kingdom,
for their every being breathes Jesus.
Blessed are their lives so entwined in the Holy Eucharist,
for without, they would cease to exist.

Blessed are those hands that hold Jesus,
so carefully, so lovingly and so devoutly.
Blessed are those hands that raise Him up,
for our healing and redemption are in those hands.

Blessed are they, Mother's special children,
for they are in the likeness of the Pieta.
Blessed are they who behold the miracle at the altar,
for they are the witness to our faith.

Blessed are the words they speak,
a guiding path and lamp to our feet.

Blessed are they for the prayers they pray,
and the sacrifices for us they make.

Blessed are they, for without them
we would cease to exist.
Blessed are they, the bearers of Christ's light,
who guide our souls from dark to bright.

Blessed are they, the bridge to grace,
connecting us with His divine embrace.
Blessed are they who stand in the breach,
to draw us nearer to Heaven's reach.

Guided By Saints

In the tapestry of faith, the saints surround,
in their holy whispers, I feel love abound.
Their lives, a beacon, guiding my way,
in trials and triumphs, they light up the grey.
I turn to you, dear saints, with hope in my heart,
for in your example, my journey can start.

In the quiet of my heart, I seek your light,
St. Dominic Savio, shining so bright.
With a youthful spirit, you walked the path,
in joy and laughter, you felt His wrath.
Your simple faith inspires my days,
to live with love in all my ways.

St. Therese of the Child Jesus, so small,
in your little way, you answer the call.
With petals scattered, your love takes flight,
in every act, you share His light.
Teach me to trust in the grace of the day,
to find joy in small things along the way.

St. John of the Cross, a mystic so wise,
in the dark night, my spirit will rise.
Your words of union, a path I pursue,
to find God's presence in all that I do.

Guide me through trials, lead me to peace,
in the depths of my soul, let my worries cease.

St. Teresa of Avila, a fortress of prayer,
in your words of wisdom, I find solace there.
You showed me the way to the heart of the Lord,
in silence and stillness, His love is poured.
Help me to seek Him in every breath,
to find His presence even in death.

As I journey through life, your spirits entwine,
with each step I take, your guidance I find.
In moments of doubt, when shadows draw near,
I call on your names, and I hold you dear.
With faith in my heart, I strive to ascend,
to walk in your footsteps, my heavenly friends.

In prayers I whisper, I feel your embrace,
a bond that transcends time and space.
With each saintly vision, I am drawn ever near,
in your holy presence, I find no fear.
So, lead me with love, through joy and strife,
With you as my guides, I embrace this life.

In Her Sacred Gaze (In Memory Of Mother Vincent SIC)

In the quiet moments, I remember her well,
my mother's aunt, a saintly soul.
A nun devoted, under Christ's sweet spell,
with each gentle act, she made my heart whole.
Sisters of the Imitation of Christ, she walked with grace,
her gaze held low, yet focused on the skies.
In every step, I could see her embrace
of a life in prayer where true love lies.
On journeys far, her eyes would look beyond,
a sign of the prayers she silently spoke.
In her presence, I felt an unbroken bond,
as she gathered us close, love's gentle cloak.

'Do your chores, my children, with joy in your heart,
offer each task as a gift to the Lord'.
'In every small duty, play your part'.
'Say the indulgent prayers; let your faith be stored'.
She taught us the path of St. Therese,
to find holiness in the little things.

In her wisdom, our worries would ease,
as she showed us how joy in service springs.
I miss her guidance, her loving embrace,
the way she reminded me to look for the light.
Though she now dwells in heaven's grace,
I ask her to pray for me each day and night.
Her spirit still lingers, a beacon of love,
In moments of doubt, I feel her near.
I know she watches from the heights above,
with a gaze that whispers, 'Do not fear'.
In the sacred lessons she left in my soul,
I strive to embody her selfless ways.
With her prayers as my guide, I feel whole.
Walking the path where her love always stays.

The Zeal Of Mar Ivanios

A flame sparked deep within his heart,
not for comfort, not for ease,
but for truth, pure and undivided,
a path few dared to see.

With eyes set on unity's vision,
he walked a road of sacrifice,
leaving behind the known and cherished,
for a dream he held as priceless.

To bring the Church to its fullness,
to restore what time had worn,
he crossed boundaries, broke traditions,
trusting God, from whom all is born.

In silence and in prayer he laboured,
each step an offering of grace,
his mission clear, his spirit steadfast,
through every trial, he embraced.

He carried Christ's light to his people,
a shepherd's heart, a servant's soul,
not seeking honour, wealth or title,
but unity, his one true goal.

Even in the face of rejection,
his zeal burned brighter still,
for he knew the cost of following
the path of God's will.

Today, we walk in the light he kindled,
a Church renewed in faith and love,
the vision of Mar Ivanios enduring,
his zeal blessed by God above.

On His Wings

I felt so low, felt so miserable.
I knew I had to go through this
for only a short while.
Yet I dragged myself through the day,
praying that it would end today.
My eyes too heavy, yet there was no sleeping.
My heart so stiff, yet there was no crying.

But now I rejoice, for those dark forests are way below me.
When I look from here, they only look like a small spot,
for the Lord has lifted me up on His wings,
through the highest mountains, through the clouds.
What a thrill to have the air fly on my face!
What a joy to catch a cloud and reach out for the stars!
My joyride has just begun, and I rejoice.

For the Lord who heard my cries has answered,
turning my sorrow into radiant light.
He has set my feet on solid ground,
and His love makes my spirit take flight.
No longer bound by the chains of despair,

His grace surrounds me everywhere.
With each beat of my heart, I praise His name,
for in His mercy, I am never the same.

Now I soar, where once I crawled.
By His strength, I am lifted, never to fall.
And though the journey is far from done,
in His embrace, the victory's won.

A Reason To Celebrate

I do not know what today holds for me.
But I know that I am the righteous,
and Your favour covers me like a shield.
I do not know what this moment will give me.
I do not know what this trial will make me.
But I do know that Your love surrounds me.
I do know that Your arms are open wide,
and You are blessing me.
So I choose now to celebrate,
for Your love is so immensely great.
I do not need to see the end of the road,
for I know You walk beside me, lifting the load.
When the storms rage, I will not be afraid,
for I trust in the plans that You have already
made.
Your goodness and mercy follow me all my days,
In every step, I will offer You praise.
Even when shadows try to hide Your light,
I choose to trust; I choose to fight.
For You are the strength when I am weak,
Your voice is the hope that I always seek.
And though the future may be unknown,
I rest in the truth that I am never alone.
So today, I lift my hands and sing,
for every moment, Your grace You bring.

With joy in my heart, I walk through the gate,
for in Your presence, I have a reason to celebrate.
I celebrate the air I breathe,
the gift of life You freely give.
I celebrate the battles You have already won.
The victory is mine, and the race is run.
Even when I cannot yet see,
I know You are making a way for me.
So I choose now to lift my voice,
for in Your promises, I rejoice.

Star Of Wonder

A star that shines through every tear,
in moments when I feel unclear.
It led the wise to Bethlehem's night,
but now it guides me through my fight.
I have seen its glow when I'm alone,
a quiet light that gently shows
the way when paths are steep and hard,
it lifts me up when I am scared.
Through struggles deep, I look above,
and find that star wrapped in His love.
When doubts press in and hope feels thin,
it reminds me of where I have always been.
It is not just a light in ancient skies,
it is the voice I hear when my spirit cries.
It walks with me when I feel low.
Whispers, 'Child, I will help you grow'.
In sleepless nights and restless days,
it is there with me, through life's haze.
The star that pulled me from despair,
and taught me God is always there.
Each step I take, each fear I face,
the star renews me with its grace.
It is not just for wise men from afar,
it is my lifeline, my guiding star.
When I have been broken, torn and bruised,

this star's light never was refused.
It healed the wounds I could not see,
and kept its glow inside of me.
This star of wonder is my own,
it has been with me, though never shown.
Through every twist and every fall,
it leads me back to God's great call.
So, as I walk, though roads are long,
I know this star will keep me strong.
It is His light shining in my heart,
from His love, I will never part.

The Lord, Our One And Mighty God

The Lord our God, the only One,
before all time, beneath the sun.
In boundless power, He reigns supreme,
the source of life, the timeless stream.

Omnipotent, His strength prevails,
in whispers soft or mighty gales.
From mountains high to oceans deep,
His watchful care will never sleep.

Omniscient One, who knows all things,
from vastness wide to smallest wings.
He sees the heart, discerns each thought,
the Master's hand in all we have sought.

Omnipresent, here and there,
in every breath, in every prayer.
No place too distant, dark or far,
for He is near, our guiding star.

Majestic Lord, beyond compare,
in light and love, forever there.
Unchanging God, both near and high–

the One we worship and glorify.

Our hearts declare with reverence deep,
the Lord alone, our souls to keep.
Our one true God, eternal, wise,
whose glory fills both earth and skies.

Wearing God's Armour

Today, I prepare myself with strength,
putting on the armour God has given.
Truth is the belt I wrap around me,
keeping me steady as I stand.
Righteousness guards my heart like armour,
reminding me to walk in what is right.

Peace covers my steps as I go,
giving me courage to face the day.
With each step, I am ready to share
the hope that guides my path.
I stand firmly in God's love,
grounded in peace and not fear.

I hold up faith like a shield,
trusting it will block any harm.
When challenges come, I know I am not alone;
God is near and will fight for me.
Even when darkness surrounds,
I trust God sees me through.

Salvation guards my mind like a helmet,
protecting me from doubts and fears.
In His promises, I find my strength,
knowing I am safe with Him.

No lie can shake me; no worry can stay,
for in His care, I am secure.

In my hand, I hold the Spirit's sword–
God's Word, my guide and strength.
When I feel lost, I listen for His voice,
finding light and wisdom there.
Through each moment, I lean on truth,
knowing His words lead my way.

With this armour, I face the day,
prepared for whatever comes.
In my tasks and in my trials,
God's strength goes with me.
Step by step, I move forward,
trusting in the One who leads me.

A Heart Awakened By The Eucharist

As I kneel before the altar,
I feel a hush settle over the room,
the air thick with holy anticipation.
Heaven meets Earth in this sacred space,
the angels gather, their wings brushing softly,
Mother Mary's gaze guiding my heart.

In this moment of transformation,
Bread and Wine become more than they seem,
the mystery unfolds, a divine embrace,
Jesus is here, Body and Blood,
a gift of love poured out for me,
the world fades away in this holy light.

With every whispered prayer,
I sense the saints surrounding me,
their faith a beacon in my own darkness,
each one a reminder of the journey,
each life a testament to His grace,
I am not alone in this sacred moment.

The priest lifts the host,
his hands trembling with reverence,

words of consecration echo in my soul,
'This is my Body and Blood, given for you',
I feel the weight of His love,
drawing me closer, deeper into His heart.

In the cup of salvation,
I taste the richness of His mercy,
the warmth of forgiveness flowing through,
I am washed clean, renewed in spirit,
each sip a promise of eternal life,
a reminder that I am His beloved.

As I receive Him, I close my eyes,
the world outside falls away,
I am enveloped in His peace,
a moment of stillness in chaos,
the miracle of the Eucharist lives within,
transforming my heart, my mind, my life.

The angels rejoice; their songs fill the air,
Mother Mary smiles with gentle pride,
the saints lift their voices in harmony,
and I am part of this divine communion,
a family bound by love,
the Body and Blood of Christ, a living testament.

In the quiet after communion,
I feel His presence linger,

His love wrapping around me like a cloak,
in this sacred intimacy, I find strength,
to face the world with renewed courage,
to share His light, His love, His peace.

I leave the altar transformed,
carrying the miracle within–
the Eucharist, a flame igniting my soul,
calling me to be His hands and feet,
to serve, to love, to bring hope,
for in the miracle of the Eucharist, I am made whole.

Lady Of Sorrows: My Refuge

A prophet's words, sharp as a blade,
foretold her grief that would never fade.
In doubt's shadow, I often tread,
fearing paths where hope seems dead.
Yet she whispers, 'Trust the plan',
her silent strength, my fears unman.
In her embrace, I stand renewed,
Her faith in God, my fortitude.

Exile's road, through desert sands,
fleeing wrath with trembling hands.
Like her, I have wandered, lost, displaced,
searching solace in trials faced.
Her steady courage lights my way,
a guiding star through night to day.
With her, I find the strength to stand,
a refugee in God's safe land.

Three days she sought, her heart in despair,
her Son, her joy, was no longer there.
I too have lost what I hold dear,
wrestling with silence, consumed by fear.
Her patience teaches me to wait,
to trust God's timing, not tempt fate.
When life seems void and answers hide,

her faith-filled search stays by my side.

Her eyes met His on that bitter road,
a silent exchange of love bestowed.
I have seen my own crosses loom ahead,
and faltered under the weight of dread.
But in her gaze, I find resolve,
A love that bids my fears dissolve.
With each step forward, though burdened still,
she leads me gently to God's will.

Beneath the cross, her heart was torn,
her Son's last breath, her soul forlorn.
I have stood by dreams as they breathed their last,
grieving the weight of a broken past.
Yet her surrender to God's decree
teaches me to let pain set me free.
Through her sorrow, a strength I find,
a love that heals, unbinds my mind.

His lifeless form, in her arms lay,
the price of love, too high to pay.
I have held regrets, cold as stone,
clinging to guilt, too scared to atone.
But her acceptance bids me see,
grace flows through loss, unceasingly.
In her sorrow, I lay my blame,
and rise anew in love's pure flame.

A tomb was sealed, her hope confined,
yet faith endured in her heart and mind.
When all seems lost and darkness reigns,
I cry to her in my silent pains.
Her trust proclaims, 'New life will rise',
a promise etched in her tear-filled eyes.
Through her grief, I am taught to believe,
That joy is born when hearts conceive.

Lady of Sorrows, my solace be,
your pierced heart delivers me.
Through every trial, you light my night,
transforming wounds with heaven's light.
Each sword that pierced your tender soul
has healed my heart and made me whole.
With you, I walk through joy and strife,
toward Christ, my Saviour, my eternal life.

Finding The Divine In Everyday Life

In the stillness of dawn,
as the sun peeks through my window,
I breathe in the soft light,
a reminder that each day is a gift.

In my morning coffee's warmth,
I find solace in the steam rising,
the aroma wraps around me,
a moment of peace before the rush.

As I step outside, I pause,
listening to the song of the birds,
their melodies weave through my heart,
calling me to notice the beauty around.

In the laughter of children playing,
I see joy in their carefree spirits,
each giggle a celebration of life,
a glimpse of innocence, a sacred echo.

During the chaos of the day,
when tasks seem to pile endlessly,
I search for a moment to breathe,

to feel His presence in the mundane.

In the simple act of folding laundry,
I find prayers hidden in the fabric,
each piece a reminder of love,
woven into the rhythm of daily life.

In the embrace of a dear friend,
I experience grace wrapped in warmth,
a shared moment, a sacred bond,
where hearts connect and spirits lift.

At the dinner table, surrounded by family,
I savour the laughter and stories shared,
each bite a blessing, each smile a treasure,
the ordinary becomes extraordinary.

As the sun sets, painting the sky,
I pause to reflect on the day's journey,
finding gratitude in the smallest details,
the sacred woven through every moment.

In the quiet of the evening,
I lay my head down, heart full,
knowing that God is in the little things,
turning the ordinary into the divine.

I carry these sacred moments with me,

like treasures tucked in my heart,
reminding me that every day holds grace,
if only I have eyes to see and believe.

Immaculate Tabernacle

O spotless dawn, creation's crown,
in you, no shadow could cast you down.
Conceived in grace, untouched by stain,
a Living Ark for heaven's reign.
The God of all chose you to bear,
His Word made flesh, beyond compare.
Immaculate Mother, pure and true,
your heart prepared the path anew.

Yet hearts that doubt this sacred grace
lose sight of love's most radiant face.
What sorrow dwells in those who deny
the gift that lifts the soul to fly!
To doubt your purity is to miss,
the foretaste of eternal bliss.
For in your 'Yes', salvation's key,
unlocked the gates for you and me.

You are the tabernacle bright,
the living host of heaven's light.
In you, the Bread of Life took form,
to calm the seas and still the storm.
As Christ now dwells in Eucharist's glow,
your womb once held what we now know.
The same divine, the same embrace,

revealed in sacramental grace.

Each time I kneel before the Bread,
your mystery lingers, deeply wed.
For just as God chose you alone,
He makes His home in hearts His own.
The tabernacle, veiled in gold,
reflects your purity of old.
Both house the Saviour, humble, concealed,
yet through them, God's great love revealed.

Blessed are they who humbly believe,
the truths the faithful soul receives.
To grasp the mystery, rich and wide,
one must let faith, not pride, abide.
For doubters walk in shadowed loss,
rejecting grace at such great cost.
But those who trust in heaven's decree
shall taste the joy of eternity.

Immaculate Mother, teach me to see,
your purity's bond with the Eucharist's plea.
That every Mass renews the day,
when God through you prepared His way.
Your womb and altar, both divine,
unveil the Saviour's love sublime.
O spotless Ark, God's chosen shrine,
your mystery calls this heart of mine.

May those who doubt be drawn by grace,
to find in you Christ's dwelling place.
And through the Eucharist, may they see,
the depth of God's humility.
Immaculate one, pure and blessed,
in you, God's love is manifest.
Tabernacle of the Word made flesh,
your faith renews, your grace refreshes.

9 789367 397695

Printed by Libri Plureos GmbH in Hamburg, Germany